HEY HUMAN...!

PUBLISHED AND DISTRIBUTED BY
VICTION WORKSHOP LTD

viction:ary™

VICTION WORKSHOP LTD
UNIT C, 7/F, SEABRIGHT PLAZA, 9-23 SHELL STREET
NORTH POINT, HONG KONG SAR
WWW.VICTIONARY.COM   WE@VICTIONARY.COM

 @VICTIONWORKSHOP   @VICTIONWORKSHOP
Bē @VICTIONARY   @VICTIONARY

EDITED, DESIGNED AND PRODUCED BY VICTION:ARY
COVER IMAGE BY NYANGSONGI
CREATIVE DIRECTION: VICTOR CHEUNG
DESIGN: LEANNE LEE / EDITORIAL: YL LIM, YNES FILLEUL
COORDINATION: LEANNE LEE / PRODUCTION: BRYAN LEUNG

SECOND EDITION
©2023, 2024 VICTION WORKSHOP LTD
ISBN 978-988-75666-7-0
PRINTED AND BOUND IN CHINA

Felinity

AN ANTHOLOGY OF
✳ CAT ILLUSTRATIONS FROM ✳
AROUND THE WORLD

What else can we say about cats – endlessly fascinating creatures that have been humanity's trusty companions and entertainers for centuries? With their mysterious and graceful air, inquisitive and independent nature, as well as their unpredictable and unwittingly funny antics, cats have captured our hearts since the beginning of their domestication, having been documented by countless storytellers, artists, writers, poets, and photographers throughout history.

From playfully mischievous kittens to elegant and dignified older cats, Felinity is a visual compendium of stunning and enchanting illustrations that embody the beguiling charm that all felines seem to possess. Be it their bewitching eyes that see in the dark, delicate whiskers that guide their path, or camouflage pelts that boast a plethora of colours and patterns, these descendants of wildcats, tigers, and leopards are intriguing creatures on their own simply with their small but mighty physique.

Moreover, cats have a way of captivating us beyond the beauty of their physical form. In our busy and chaotic lives, our feline friends offer us respite with their carefree demeanour, reminding us to slow down and appreciate the simple pleasures in life. Their calming presence and soft purrs bring comfort and solace while they are in our company, soothing us after a long day of facing the world. Through their curious gaze, cats seem to paw their way into the depths of our souls, forging a bond not unlike the connection that our ancestors once shared with their feline companions.

In Felinity, you will find that each page is a testament to the creativity and talent of artists and illustrators who have been inspired by the feline form. Their interpretations showcase a range of styles, from the fine strokes of a paintbrush and realistic renderings that capture the intricate details of a cat's fur and whiskers, to whimsically abstract representations that evoke the feline spirit. Ultimately, each illustration is a unique expression of the artist's love for these curious creatures.

In addition to the artwork, this book is also peppered with fascinating, little-known facts that will further endear you to the extraordinary animals. These pages will also delve into the myths, legends, and cultural references that have surrounded cats, shedding light on their enduring presence in our collective consciousness.

Whether you are a passionate cat lover, an art enthusiast, or simply someone who appreciates the beauty of the animal world, we hope this book will delight and inspire you with the lovingly-drawn details found within. As you turn each page, may you feel a sense of wonder and joy, while developing an even deeper appreciation for the lovely creatures that grace our homes and hearts.

To enjoy this book to the fullest, we invite you, dear reader, to help yourself to a drink of your choice and sit back in your favourite reading area, perhaps curled up with your own special feline friend, as you indulge in every meow-ment of bliss!

Nyangsongi

Nyangsongi is the pen name of Keumjin Song, an artist who describes herself as the butler of a fat cat. Whether they are cool and aloof or adorable and friendly, she enjoys creating heartwarming caricatures of cats in various daily episodes.

A BIT, A BIT MORE INSIDE!
250MM X 250MM, MIXED MEDIA

I FEEL LISTLESS :-(
250MM X 250MM, MIXED MEDIA

THE WARMEST PLACE
250MM X 250MM, MIXED MEDIA

IT'S DANGEROUS OUTSIDE THE STOVE
250MM X 250MM, MIXED MEDIA

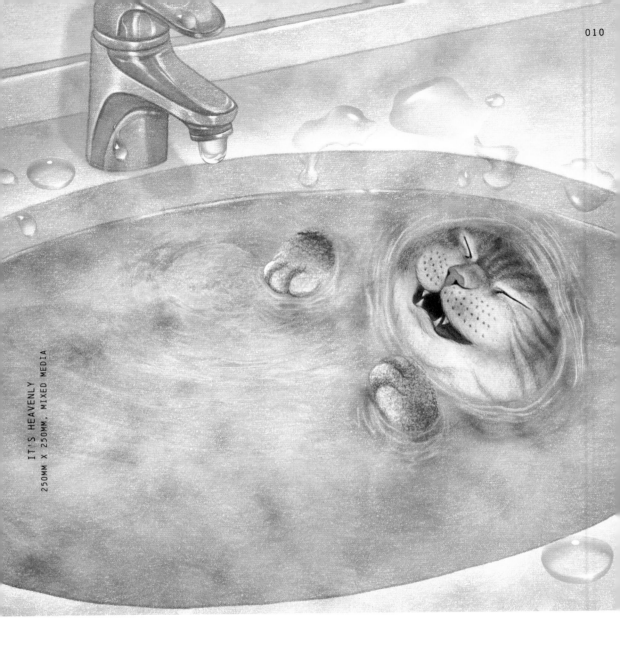

IT'S HEAVENLY
250MM X 250MM. MIXED MEDIA

MY PRIVATE BATHTUB
250MM X 250MM, MIXED MEDIA

TROUBLEMAKER
250MM X 250MM, MIXED MEDIA

MEDIUM-RARE? OR WELL-DONE?
250MM X 250MM, MIXED MEDIA

LOVERS OF BOX
250MM X 250MM, MIXED MEDIA

LOVERS OF BOX
250MM X 250MM, MIXED MEDIA

THE PERFECT SEAT
250MM X 250MM, MIXED MEDIA

I AM NOT FAT, THE WALL IS JUST TOO SMALL
250MM X 250MM, MIXED MEDIA

A LUCKY DREAM
250MM X 250MM, MIXED MEDIA

Kae Higuchi

Kae Higuchi creates paintings and prints with tempera and oil. She occasionally fosters and finds families for cats, while living with 8 of her own in Japan. Kae is also the founder of "cat&dog&me", a volunteer organisation for dog and cat welfare.

"NO CAT, NO LIFE."
180MM X 140MM, TEMPERA, OIL, PENCIL, WOOD PANEL

PORTRAIT OF A CAT "BOCCHAN"
121MM X 101MM, TEMPERA, OIL, PENCIL, PLYWOOD

PORTRAIT OF A CAT "TILL-SAMA"
121MM X 101MM, TEMPERA, OIL, PENCIL, PLYWOOD

CAT'S GARDEN
332MM X 332MM, TEMPERA, OIL, PENCIL, WOOD PANEL

M MURO-CHAN
146MM X 112MM, TEMPERA, OIL, PENCIL, PLYWOOD

N NICO-CHAN
145MM X 121MM, TEMPERA, OIL, PENCIL, PLYWOOD

LEMON GIRL AND ROLL BOY
140MM X 180MM, TEMPERA, OIL, PENCIL, WOOD PANEL

CERTAINTY PROPORTIONAL TO WEIGHT
257MM X 183MM. TEMPERA. OIL. PENCIL. WOOD PANEL

Amelia Art

Amelia H-Jastrzębska is an oil painter who hones her cute and whimsical style with a bittersweet touch of darkness. After studying at the Academy of Fine Arts in Poland, she set up her own studio in the countryside, where nature serves as a valuable source of inspiration for her work.

ANOTHER DARK CLOUD
250MM X 250MM, OIL, CANVAS

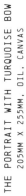

THE PORTRAIT WITH TURQUOISE BOW
205MM X 255MM, OIL, CANVAS

THE SHAPE OF MY PRIVATE PIECE OF THE WORLD
250MM X 250MM, OIL, CANVAS

"❦I think [cats] are quite mysterious in a way that is difficult to explain, and only through art can we come close to understanding them. For me, there is something just so fascinating about cats."

TABBY CAT PORTRAIT WITH A BLACK TEAR

205MM X 255MM, OIL, CANVAS

THE PORTRAIT WITH THE MYSTERIOUS TREE
205MM X 255MM, OIL, CANVAS

WE LOST IN THE JOURNEY
205MM X 255MM, OIL, CANVAS

Naoko Shono

Naoko Shono is an illustrator and picture book author whose work has been published by Kodansha. Besides the "Lucchio & Frifri" series and "The North Pole Circus", she has also illustrated for "The Second Bad Guy" and BRUTUS magazine's "I Like" series covers.

BAG OF FISH
132MM X 202MM, ACRYLIC GOUACHE, WATERCOLOUR PAPER

SKATERS

206MM X 137MM, ACRYLIC GOUACHE, WATERCOLOUR PAPER

BALL-RIDING

138MM X 206MM, ACRYLIC GOUACHE, WATERCOLOUR PAPER

ELIZABETH COLLAR

146MM X 214MM. ACRYLIC GOUACHE, WATERCOLOUR PAPER

WEEPING MIMI
137MM X 204MM, ACRYLIC GOUACHE, WATERCOLOUR PAPER

"I always imagine when I see cats roaming around the street that they're probably on their way to their secret magical world that us humans can't see with our naked eye, and if I'm lucky, I can turn those daydreams into illustrations."

THE WORLD OF LUCCHIO & FRIFRI
206MM X 137MM, ACRYLIC GOUACHE, WATERCOLOUR PAPER

MY FRIEND
132MM X 201MM, ACRYLIC GOUACHE, WATERCOLOUR PAPER

LADRI DI BICICLETTE
140MM X 190MM, ACRYLIC GOUACHE, WATERCOLOUR PAPER

CHRISTMAS
426MM X 263MM, ACRYLIC GOUACHE, WATERCOLOUR PAPER

Kamwei Fong

Artist Kamwei Fong is known for his poetic, humorous, imaginative, playful, and dream-like creations. Besides receiving global recognition, his work has also been exhibited at Salon des Beaux Arts in Paris and Art Expo Malaysia in Kuala Lumpur.

THE FURRY THING - KIKI NO.2
297MM X 210MM, FINE LINER, PAPER

THE FURRY THING - BONDING NO.2
297MM X 210MM, FINE LINER, PAPER

THE FURRY THING — BONDING NO.3
297MM X 210MM, FINE LINER, PAPER

THE FURRY THING - KITTY NO.39
210MM X 297MM, FINE LINER, PAPER

THE FURRY THING – KITTY NO.59
210MM X 297MM, FINE LINER, PAPER

THE FURRY THING – KITTY NO.95 – BE NICE
297MM X 210MM, FINE LINER, PAPER

Be nice.

THE FURRY THING - KITTY NO.94 - BE A CAT
297MM X 210MM, FINE LINER, PAPER

Be a cat.

THE FURRY THING – KITTY NO.113
297MM X 210MM, FINE LINER, PAPER

THE FURRY THING - KITTY NO.72
297MM X 210MM, FINE LINER, PAPER

THE FURRY THING — IN THE WONDERFURRYLAND NO.4
297MM X 210MM, FINE LINER, PAPER

DID YOU KNOW?

ALTHOUGH CATS USE THEIR **TAIL** TO **COMMUNICATE** WITH US AND BALANCE THEMSELVES, THEY CAN LIVE WITHOUT ONE – THEY LEARN TO COMPENSATE FOR THE LOSS WITH THEIR POWERFUL **BACK LEGS**.

WHILE HUMANS HAVE **206 BONES**, FELINES HAVE A TOTAL OF **230 BONES** IN THEIR AGILE AND FLEXIBLE BODIES.

CATS USUALLY SPEND **1/3** OF THEIR WAKING LIVES **GROOMING** THEMSELVES AND ANOTHER **1/3 NAPPING** TO CONSERVE ENERGY.

CATS CAN GENERALLY **SQUEEZE INTO ANY HOLE** AS LONG AS THEIR HEAD FITS BECAUSE THEIR COLLARBONES ARE BUILT DIFFERENTLY, MAKING THEM SEEM LIKE **LIQUID!**

THE **MAINE COON** IS THE WORLD'S **LARGEST** PEDIGREE CAT, WHICH CAN WEIGH MORE THAN **9 KGS** AND GROW UP TO **1 METRE** LONG!

THE **LOUDEST** CAT PURR WAS RECORDED AT **67.8DB(A)**, WHICH IS ALMOST AS LOUD AS A **VACUUM CLEANER** OR WASHING MACHINE!

DOMESTIC CATS SHARE **95.6%** OF THEIR DNA WITH THEIR **TIGER** ANCESTORS.

WHILE THEY BECOME MOST **ACTIVE** AT DAWN AND DUSK, CATS ARE USUALLY **ASLEEP** FOR **12-16 HOURS** A DAY.

THE **DOMESTIC CAT** LIVES FOR AN AVERAGE OF **12-16 YEARS**, BUT SOME LUCKY ELDERLY FELINES CAN LIVE WELL INTO THEIR **20'S**.

DUE TO A **GENETIC MUTATION**, CATS ARE IMMUNE TO THE TASTE OF **SWEETNESS**, BUT CAN STILL TASTE SALTY, SOUR, BITTER, AND UMAMI FLAVOURS.

Moe Higuchi

Upon graduating from Aoyamajuku, Tokyo-based Aichi native
Moe Higuchi worked at design firms and web design agencies
before becoming an illustrator. She focuses on editorial and book
design, and mainly uses marker pens,
coloured pencils, and Photoshop in her work.

TEA TIME
280MM X 280MM, MARKER PEN, COLOURED PENCILS

WATERING
190MM X 270MM, MARKER PEN, COLOURED PENCILS, ACRYLIC

Higuchi Moe

GO TO BED

190MM X 270MM, MARKER PEN, COLOURED PENCILS, ACRYLIC

"One of the most intriguing aspect of cats is that we have no way of knowing what they are thinking, which I believe is what attracts so many people to them."

CATS DANCE
257MM X 364MM, MARKER PEN, COLOURED PENCILS

TO AIR OUT BOOKS
210MM X 297MM, MARKER PEN, COLOURED PENCILS

CATS AND BOOK
190MM X 270MM, MARKER PEN, COLOURED PENCILS, ACRYLIC

Higuchi Moe
2020

TOOTHBRUSHING
210MM X 297MM, MARKER PEN, COLOURED PENCILS

ABSENCE OF MIND
148MM X 210MM, DIGITAL

Sora Mizusawa

Hakodate-born Sora Mizusawa is an illustrator based in Tokyo
and a member of the Tokyo Illustrators Society who graduated from the
Vantan Design Institute and MJ Illustrations. Her work has been published,
nominated, and awarded in various competitions over the years.

GOOD MORNING, AND THIS WONDERFUL WORLD
182MM X 257MM, WATERCOLOUR, PAPER

FROM THE CARTOON "CHUBBY"
297MM X 210MM, WATERCOLOUR, PAPER, PUBLISHER: KIKEN

CHUBBY
297MM X 210MM, WATERCOLOUR, PAPER

"I have spent time with cats since childhood, so painting cats comes naturally to me."

I'M THE REAL SLACKER
182MM X 257MM, WATERCOLOUR, PAPER, PUBLISHER: KIKEN

SURROUNDED BY LOCAL PUNKS

515MM X 364MM, WATERCOLOUR, PAPER, PUBLISHER: KIKEN

Lanmita

Lanmita was born in Bangkok and graduated in communication design. She studied various painting techniques after developing a strong interest in analogue drawing and works mainly with acrylic, along with crayon, oil pastel, and coloured pencils. Her art is usually inspired by nature, women, and animals.

QUILT CUTE
297MM X 232MM, ACRYLIC, PAPER

REAL-LIFE SITUATION
297MM X 267MM, ACRYLIC, PAPER

BLACK COFFEE IS BROWN
297MM X 221MM, ACRYLIC, COLOURED PENCILS, PAPER

FEELING FESTIVE
297MM X 210MM, ACRYLIC, PAPER

WHITE CATS
297MM X 210MM, ACRYLIC, PAPER

SHOYU
297MM X 210MM, ACRYLIC, PAPER

Tomoko Takahashi

Tomoko Takahashi is an Osaka-born, US-based Japanese artist who creates whimsical and colourful depictions of animals, plants, and women in a unique, daydreamy style that stems from her subconsciousness. Her signature cat series showcases a playful and humorous worldview with a distinctive perspective.

CAT'S PARADISE
279.4MM X 279.4MM, ACRYLIC, PAPER

CAT'S ADVENTURE
279.4MM X 355.6MM, ACRYLIC, PAPER

CAT ROAMING NEIGHBOURHOOD
279.4MM X 355.6MM, ACRYLIC, PAPER

BLACK CAT IN PUMPKIN GARDEN
279.4MM X 279.4MM, ACRYLIC, PAPER

CAT WITH FROG IN LOTUS GARDEN
279.4MM X 279.4MM, ACRYLIC, PAPER

BLACK CAT IN THE MOONLIGHT
279.4MM X 355.6MM, ACRYLIC, PAPER

WHITE CAT WITH FLOWERS IN THE FOREST
279.4MM X 355.6MM, ACRYLIC, PAPER

YUME THE CAT
279.4MM X 355.6MM, ACRYLIC, PAPER

Maori Mihata

Maori Mihata has been obsessed with cats ever since living
with them when she was 6 years old. She currently paints and creates
three-dimensional work such as matryoshka dolls and kokeshi
dolls. She also showcases her world of funny and lovable cats on her
website, Marupoleland.

LOOKING FOR YOU FAR AWAY
180MM X 140MM, ACRYLIC GOUACHE, SOFT PASTELS

HAPPY BOYS PICNIC
227MM X 158MM, ACRYLIC GOUACHE

OUR WAY HOME
273MM X 220MM, ACRYLIC GOUACHE, SOFT PASTELS

BECAUSE I'M THE MAIN STAGE
180MM X 140MM, ACRYLIC GOUACHE, SOFT PASTELS

HELLO, HELLO, THE SUN IS COMING SOON
227MM X 158MM, ACRYLIC GOUACHE, SOFT PASTELS

TOYS ARE FALLING FROM THE SKY
227MM X 158MM, ACRYLIC GOUACHE, SOFT PASTELS

I WISH FOR

227MM X 158MM, ACRYLIC GOUACHE, SOFT PASTELS

Yuzu Kato

Yuzu Kato specialises in Japanese-style acrylic paintings based on the theme of animals or cats. On rare occasions, she also uses pencils, oils, and draws manga. She enjoys creating updates about her cat son, Senna, and runs her own web shop, Yuzu no Mori.

EVERYONE LOOKS LIKE A CAT
180MM X 230MM, OIL

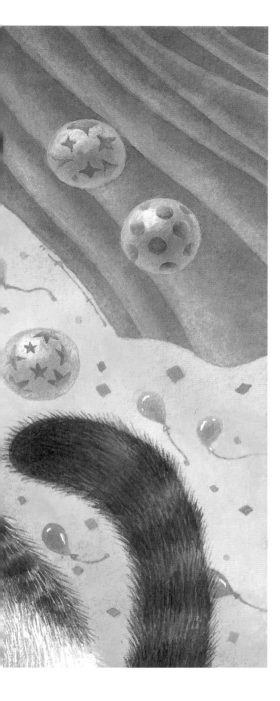

LET'S START
180MM X 230MM, OIL

GIRLS' CLUB
180MM X 230MM, OIL

COAT IN TIGER PATTERN
180MM X 230MM, OIL

WON'T YOU PLAY WITH ME
180MM X 230MM, OIL

SAMURAI CAT
180MM X 230MM, OIL

VOICE OF THE FOREST
180MM X 230MM, OIL

POWER FROM TIGER
180MM X 230MM, OIL

Anna Maia

Anna Maia was born in 1983 and grew up in Stockholm, where she developed her love for painting. She has spent over a decade as a tattoo artist and currently creates Japanese-inspired artwork with a focus on cats and florals, reflecting her fascination with Japanese culture, language, and art.

KITSUNE CAT
390MM X 560MM, DIGITAL

WHITE CAT
390MM X 560MM, DIGITAL

DOWNSTREAM
390MM X 560MM, DIGITAL

THE WATER BOWL
390MM X 560MM, DIGITAL

FOLDED PAPER CRANE
390MM X 560MM, DIGITAL

CROWS BLACK CAT
390MM X 560MM, DIGITAL

RABBIT KITTEN
390MM X 560MM, DIGITAL

TEAPOT KITTEN
390MM X 560MM, DIGITAL

RED TEAPOT
390MM X 560MM, DIGITAL

1 EYES

WHILE CATS ARE COLOUR-BLIND IN RED AND GREEN HUES AND MID-SIGHTED, THEY DETECT MOTION A LOT FASTER THAN HUMANS DO.

3 WHISKERS

CATS' WHISKERS GROW IN PROPORTION TO THEIR BODY WIDTH AND ARE USED TO DETERMINE IF THEY CAN FIT INTO NARROW SPACES.

2 NOSE

A CAT'S NOSE PRINT IS LIKE FINGERPRINTS FOR HUMANS – IT IS MADE UP OF TINY RIDGES AND BUMPS THAT MAKE EACH ONE UNIQUE.

4 EARS

THE FLAP OUTSIDE A CAT'S EAR IS CALLED A HENRY'S POCKET. WHILE ITS FUNCTIONS ARE UNCLEAR, IT PROBABLY HELPS CATS DETECT HIGH-PITCHED SOUNDS.

5 FLANK

A CAT'S PRIMORDIAL POUCH ACTS AS A NUTRIENT RESERVE, PROTECTS ITS VITAL ORGANS, AND GIVES IT EXTRA STRETCHING POWER.

6 TAIL BASE

THE BASE OF A CAT'S TAIL CONTAINS MANY NERVE ENDINGS. SOME CATS ENJOY BEING SCRATCHED THERE AS IT MAKES THEM FEEL HAPPY AND RELAXED.

7 FEET

JUST LIKE CAMELS AND GIRAFFES, CATS MOVE BOTH OF THEIR RIGHT FEET BEFORE THEIR LEFT - MAKING THEM UNIQUE IN THE ANIMAL KINGDOM.

Mai Shikama

After graduating from Tokyo University of the Arts majoring in Japanese painting, Mai participated in multiple exhibitions and won awards for her work, including the Grand Prize at the 20th Shohaku Museum Exhibition. She received her Master of Arts in 2015, and is currently an associate of the Japan Art Institute.

SCARLET RED
273MM X 273MM, MINERAL PIGMENT, MUD PIGMENT,
GOLD FOIL, TOSA HEMP PAPER

TWELVE COLOURS-RUBY
158MM X 227MM. MINERAL PIGMENT, MUD PIGMENT,
SILVER FOIL, TOSA HEMP PAPER

SKY BLUE
410MM X 530MM, MINERAL PIGMENT,
MUD PIGMENT, TOSA HEMP PAPER

A GARDEN WITH NARCISSUS
500MM X 727MM, MINERAL PIGMENT, MUD PIGMENT,
GOIL FOIL, TOSA HEMP PAPER, WASHI

A WATER JUG β
530MM X 455MM, MINERAL PIGMENT, MUD PIGMENT,
KUMOHADA HEMP PAPER

"Cats are a familiar motif to me as I keep them at home. Their faces are very expressive, and the way they move is charming too."

BLUE
273MM X 160MM, MINERAL PIGMENT, MUD PIGMENT, KUMOHADA HEMP PAPER

Jinhee Yoo

Jinhee Yoo is an artist who specialises in Minhwa, a traditional Korean painting style. She loves drawing cats and lives with one named Hyang, which means "fragrance" in Korean. She dreams of a world where animals and people can live happily together.

I'LL GIVE YOU HAPPINESS. SO, BE MY BUTLER
290MM X 290MM, ORIENTAL PAINT, HANJI
(TRADITIONAL KOREAN PAPER)

KKAMNYANG
300MM X 300MM, ORIENTAL PAINT, HANJI
(TRADITIONAL KOREAN PAPER)

ANGJEUNG
390MM X 310MM, ORIENTAL PAINT, HANJI
(TRADITIONAL KOREAN PAPER)

WHITE RICE KITTY
220MM X 220MM, ORIENTAL PAINT, HANJI
(TRADITIONAL KOREAN PAPER)

BLACK RICE KITTY
220MM X 220MM, ORIENTAL PAINT, HANJI
(TRADITIONAL KOREAN PAPER)

ROYALTY
420MM X 300MM, ORIENTAL PAINT, HANJI
(TRADITIONAL KOREAN PAPER)

CATS IN A PEACH PARADISE
280MM X 310MM, ORIENTAL PAINT, HANJI
(TRADITIONAL KOREAN PAPER)

CATS IN THE WATERMELON POOL
550MM X 370MM, ORIENTAL PAINT, HANJI
(TRADITIONAL KOREAN PAPER)

FRAGRANCES IN LOTUS SPA
390MM X 300MM, ORIENTAL PAINT, HANJI
(TRADITIONAL KOREAN PAPER)

BuBuCat · DavidCooksLove

BuBuCat was born from a homophone of Wen Hsiu Lin's own pets, Zuzu and David (nicknamed Bubu). Inspired by her love of cats, painting, cooking, and shopping in small markets, she always fantasises about felines in different scenarios and incorporates them into her work.

DANDELION
200MM X 290MM, WATERCOLOUR

EASTER EGG OF KING FISH
270MM X 270MM, WATERCOLOUR

RED AND GREEN EASTER EGG
260MM X 260MM, WATERCOLOUR

BROWN BEECH MUSHROOM GROVE
230MM X 230MM, WATERCOLOUR

CHILI PEPPER RAGDOLL
210MM X 170MM, WATERCOLOUR

GOBLET OF SWEET TREATS
260MM X 260MM, WATERCOLOUR

EIFFEL TOWER
160MM X 225MM, WATERCOLOUR
COMMERCIAL WORK FOR SKINCARE BRAND "BOYFRIEND"

CHAMPS ELYSEES
160MM X 225MM, WATERCOLOUR
COMMERCIAL WORK FOR SKINCARE BRAND "BOYFRIEND"

"I think cats are like finely-crafted works of art that behave in a cute manner. I often used cats as the theme of my creations in college, and I hope that their healing power can be felt as presented in my imagination."

TATTOO ARTIST
190MM X 270MM, WATERCOLOUR
PRIVATE COMMISSIONED WORK FOR "TATTOO ME"

YO-CO

YO-CO is a Japanese artist who mainly creates paintings with motifs of cats and mushrooms, using various techniques such as three-dimensional modelling, silk screens, and copperplate engravings. YO-CO also designs and sells products featuring her paintings via her web shop.

STAND BY ME
390MM X 460MM, WATERCOLOUR, PIGMENT INK, WATSON PAPER

CAT MASTER OF COFFEE SHOP
52MM X 82MM, ACRYLIC, CANVAS

THREE-STAR CHEF
52MM X 82MM, ACRYLIC, CANVAS

TEMPTATION
148MM X 148MM, COFFEE, WATERCOLOUR,
PIGMENT INK, ARCHES PAPERINK

EAT ME

MOONLIT NIGHT
148MM X 148MM, COFFEE, WATERCOLOUR,
PIGMENT INK, ARCHES PAPERINK

"Cats are bewitching, charming, beautiful, lovely, and precious all at the same time. While there may be many reasons to love cats, I personally believe logic isn't necessary to explain one's love for cats!"

ON A FULL MOON NIGHT
148MM X 148MM, COFFEE, WATERCOLOUR, PIGMENT INK, ARCHES PAPERINK

夜 のとばりが降りる頃
猫達は大忙し

STARRY NIGHT
320MM X 416MM, COFFEE, WATERCOLOUR,
PIGMENT INK, ARCHES PAPER

Starry Night

星のランプをぱちぱちと
灯して回ります

Léa Le Pivert

Based in Brest, French illustrator Léa Le Pivert offers a unique perspective in her work, thanks to her background in textile and graphic design. Her soothing illustrations are brought to life using hand-painted textures, giving her art a distinctive depth and character.

GET WELL SOON
297MM X 210MM, MIXED MEDIA, DIGITAL

READY FOR AUTUMN
254MM X 254MM, MIXED MEDIA, DIGITAL

NEW FRIEND
307MM X 307MM, MIXED MEDIA, DIGITAL

CLOUDY AFTERNOON
356MM X 356MM, MIXED MEDIA, DIGITAL

HOW TO BECOME A CAT

297MM X 210MM, MIXED MEDIA, DIGITAL

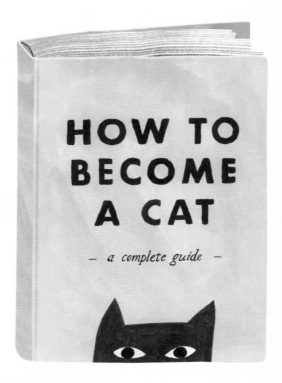

LAZY EVENING
297MM X 210MM, MIXED MEDIA, DIGITAL

Laura Agustí

Laura graduated in fine arts from the Miguel Hernández of Altea University. Focusing on illustration, she spent several years dedicated to painting and held several individual and collective exhibitions. She has also published two illustrated books. Her work of delicate lines recall romantic, historical times with a modern twist.

PENGUINCAT
297MM X 210MM, DIGITAL

CHUI
297MM X 210MM, DIGITAL

LEO
297MM X 210MM, DIGITAL

WATERMELON
297MM X 210MM, DIGITAL

BAT CAT
297MM X 210MM, DIGITAL

"I love drawing cats and their feline features, as well as their intelligent and cunning looks. I also try to convey the softness of their fur and their beauty, and hope that people feel the affection I have for them in my drawings."

BELLY UP
297MM X 210MM, DIGITAL

UNITED STATES

WHILE CATS ARE NOT NATIVE TO THE AMERICAS, 'SHIPCATS' WERE INTRODUCED BY COLONIST SHIPS AS THEY PROTECTED THE FOOD SUPPLY FROM RODENTS.

TURKEY

ISTANBUL, THE CAPITAL OF TURKEY, IS THE WORLD'S MOST CAT-FRIENDLY CITY WITH A FELINE POPULATION OF MORE THAN 150,000.

EGYPT

IT WAS ILLEGAL TO HARM OR KILL CATS IN ANCIENT EGYPT AS THEY WERE A SYMBOL OF BAST, THE GODDESS OF PROTECTION.

JAPAN

SINCE THE EDO PERIOD, SHOPS IN JAPAN WOULD INSTALL BECKONING CAT ORNAMENTS AS CALICO CATS WERE ASSOCIATED WITH GOOD LUCK.

FRANCE

A PARISIAN STRAY CAT NAMED FELICETTE WAS SENT TO SPACE AS PART OF A SPACE MISSION ON 18 OCTOBER 1963.

AUSTRALIA

THE WORLD RECORD FOR THE FATTEST CAT EVER BELONGS TO HIMMY, AN AUSSIE CAT FROM CAIRNS WHO WEIGHED 21.3KG AT HIS HEAVIEST.

The Dancing Cat

The Dancing Cat features the art of Jamie Shelman, a graduate of Rhode Island School of Design. Inspired by their plump shapes and seal-like bodies, Jamie finds cats to be the perfect form of self expression, and hopes their art captures and stirs a passion for cats within viewers.

BEAUTY QUEENS
215.9MM X 279.4MM, DIGITAL

RAGDOLL
215.9MM X 279.4MM, DIGITAL

HOUSE PLANT CAT
215.9MM X 279.4MM, DIGITAL

CALICO & TORTIE
215.9MM X 279.4MM, DIGITAL

KITCHEN CATS
356MM X 432MM, DIGITAL

STAIR CATS
480MM X 508MM, DIGITAL

PLANT KITTY
154MM X 180MM, DIGITAL

THE BONDING HOUR
203.2MM X 203.2MM, DIGITAL

Léa Chounlamountry

Léa Chounlamountry is a French illustrator and graphic designer who mainly draws cats and plants. Inspired by the calm and quirky nature of felines, she enjoys depicting them in charming situations. She also incorporates traditional elements and texture in her digital work using her experience in coloured pencils.

UNDERCOVER
2480 X 3508 PIXELS, DIGITAL

CAT AND ANTHURIUM
5846 X 4134 PIXELS, DIGITAL

CAT AND HOUSEPLANT
4724 X 4724 PIXELS, DIGITAL

CAT IN A COSY BLANKET
3508 X 2480 PIXELS, DIGITAL

LEA
CHOUN
LAMOUN
TRY

CAT AND TULIPS
3508 X 3508 PIXELS, DIGITAL

CALICO CAT AND MELON
4134 X 4134 PIXELS, DIGITAL

Alison Kolesar

Alison Kolesar grew up in Edinburgh and currently lives in New England. Inspired by nature and colour, she paints people, animals, and the natural world, using both traditional materials and digital tools. She has illustrated many books and repeated patterns that adorn clothing and other products.

TUXEDO CAT
260MM X 260MM, GOUACHE

WHITE CAT
260MM X 260MM, GOUACHE

BLACK & WHITE CAT
260MM X 260MM, GOUACHE

GINGER CAT
260MM X 260MM, GOUACHE

CALICO CAT
260MM X 260MM, GOUACHE

KITTIES AND CUSHIONS
285.75MM X 212.7MM, WATERCOLOUR, GOUACHE

BIRDIE ON MY WINDOWSILL
355MM X 279MM, COLLAGE

WHEN LIFE GIVES YOU LEMONS
355MM X 279MM, COLLAGE

"I enjoy cats on a purely aesthetic level —
their sinuous movements, amazing agility, and
frequently dainty positions that make them
quite decorative and a visual joy.
They can seem inscrutable, but I tend to give
them expressions – challenging, curious, or
smug – when I paint them."

Benedek Chen

Benedek moved to Michigan as a young child and has always loved art and animals. He studied illustration at the College for Creative Studies. After graduating and facing many challenges in his journey, he decided to focus on himself and solidify his unique art style along with his fascination for animals.

SNOW KITTENS
279.4MM X 355.6MM, COLOURED PENCILS

DIAMOND CAT 2
203.2MM X 254MM, COLOURED PENCILS

SIBERIAN CAT
279.4MM X 355.6MM, COLOURED PENCILS

TANGO CATS
457.2MM X 609.6MM, COLOURED PENCILS, GOUACHE, DIGITAL

Benedek C

Bened

THE KITTEN
203.2MM X 254MM, COLOURED PENCILS, GOUACHE, DIGITAL

DIAMOND CAT 4
203.2MM X 254MM, COLOURED PENCILS, GOUACHE

Essi Kimpimäki

Essi is a Finnish freelance illustrator based in Edinburgh. She is an avid lover of bright colours, bold shapes, as well as different textures, while her favourite drawing subjects are cats and flowers. Her whimsical illustrations are created digitally, using textured brushes for a handmade touch.

NIGHT KITTY
5000 X 6408 PIXELS, DIGITAL

MEADOW KITTY
4877 X 4877 PIXELS, DIGITAL

TEARS FOR UKRAINE
4253 X 4253 PIXELS, DIGITAL

DESERT KITTY
3536 X 5000 PIXELS, DIGITAL

DAISY CAT
3778 X 3778 PIXELS, DIGITAL

NAP
4198 X 4198 PIXELS, DIGITAL

Namasri Niumim

Namasri is an illustrator from Bangkok who lives on and off
between her home country and Oceania. She mostly works with gouache
and watercolour, and her illustrations often feature fauna and flora in
bright colours.

BECKONING CATS
209MM X 209MM, GOUACHE

BECKONING CATS
209MM X 209MM, GOUACHE

BECKONING CATS
209MM X 209MM, GOUACHE

THE THREE MUSKETEERS
182MM X 269MM, GOUACHE

"Cats are such mysterious creatures behind their cute features, and I think they cast a spell and lured me to fall in love with them. I believe that cats have special healing powers through their bright eyes and purring that can brighten up any gloomy day."

SCRATCH
210MM X 294MM, GOUACHE

JOY CAT
297MM X 210MM, GOUACHE

ACKNOWLEDGEMENTS

WE WOULD LIKE TO THANK ALL THE DESIGNERS, STUDIOS, AND
COMPANIES WHO WERE INVOLVED IN THE PRODUCTION OF THIS BOOK
FOR THEIR SIGNIFICANT CONTRIBUTION TO ITS COMPILATION. WE
WOULD ALSO LIKE TO EXPRESS OUR GRATITUDE TO ALL THE PRODUCERS
INVOLVED FOR THEIR INVALUABLE OPINIONS AND ASSISTANCE, AS
WELL AS THE PROFESSIONALS IN THE CREATIVE INDUSTRY WHO WERE
GENEROUS WITH THEIR INSIGHTS AND FEEDBACK THROUGHOUT THE
ENTIRE PRODUCTION PROCESS. LAST BUT NOT LEAST, TO THOSE WHO
MADE SPECIFIC INPUT BEHIND THE SCENES BUT WERE NOT CREDITED IN
THIS BOOK, WE ACKNOWLEDGE AND APPRECIATE ALL YOUR EFFORT AND
CONTINUOUS SUPPORT.

FUTURE EDITIONS

IF YOU WISH TO PARTICIPATE IN VICTION:ARY'S FUTURE PROJECTS
AND PUBLICATIONS, PLEASE SEND YOUR WEBSITE OR PORTFOLIO TO
WE@VICTIONARY.COM